AFTER PRÉVERT
Poems from *Paroles*

Also by J. T. Barbarese

True Does Nothing (Plume/MadHat, 2018).

Sweet Spot (Northwestern University Press, 2012).

The Black Beach (UNT Press, 2005).

A Very Small World (Orchises Press, 2005).

New Science (University of Georgia Press, 1989).

Under the Blue Moon (University of Georgia Press, 1985).

Translations:

The Children of Heracles (University of Pennsylvania Press, 1999).

AFTER PRÉVERT
Poems from *Paroles*

J. T. Barbarese

MadHat Press
Cheshire, Massachusetts

MadHat Press
PO Box 422, Cheshire MA 01225

Jacques Prévert, *Paroles* © Editions GALLIMARD, Paris, 1949

Copyright © 2022 J. T. Barbarese
All rights reserved

The Library of Congress has assigned
this edition a Control Number of
2020941994

ISBN 978-1-952335-09-9 (paperback)

Cover image: *Smoke image* by Stephen Hocking
Cover design by Marc Vincenz
Book design by MadHat Press

www.MadHat-Press.com

Published in the United States of America

Table of Contents

Prévert Now	xi
La Belle Saison	3
Nice Weather	4
Pater Noster	5
Pater Noster	7
Le Discours sur la paix	8
Toothless Argument	9
La Grasse Matinée	10
Continental Breakfast	13
Chanson des escargots qui vont à l'enterrement	16
Did You Hear the One About	18
Le Cancre	20
Class Clown	21
Il ne faut pas …	22
11th Commandment	23
Le Désespoir est assis sur un banc	24
Park Bench Sphinx	26
Page d'écriture	28
Copybook Page	30

Vous allez voir ce que vous allez voir	32
You'll See Just What You're Going to See	33
J'en ai vu plusieurs	34
Outside the V.A. Hospital	35
Presque	36
Almost	37
L'École des beaux-arts	38
Instant Art	39
Familiale	40
All in the Family	41
Le Retour au pays	42
Body Language	44
Paris at night	46
Three on a Match	47
Chez la fleuriste	48
Rolling Poem	50
Et la fête continue	52
Liberation Day	53
L'Effort humain	54
Human Condition	57
Le Cheval rouge	60
Red Horse Smile	61

Composition Française	62
Essay Question	63
Le Message	64
Theory of Narrative	65
Le Bouquet	66
Posies	67
Riviera	68
Kicking Back	71
Le Combat avec l'ange	74
Your Arms Are Too Short to Box With God	75
Notes	77
Acknowledgments	79
About the Author	81

Prévert Now

The canonical Anglo-American poetry of the twentieth century seems to have skipped what was elemental to contemporaneous European poetry: intense political engagement, at least until the arrival of the Beats, an embrace of the vernacular, and "world history" in general.

Take the major players. Eliot, the most influential of the Modernists, was dead set against any idealism except a morose, aestheticized Anglicanism that gradually took the shape of the program called the New Criticism. When asked to describe the sources of *The Waste Land*, probably by those who wondered if the title referred to the phrase 'no man's land,' the ravaged space separating the Allies from the German front lines in World War I, he replied that it was "a bit of rhythmic grumbling," his way of telling you to mind your own business. Pound emphatically believed that history was a legitimate source of poetry, but the outcome of that belief, *The Cantos*, with notable exceptions is all but unreadable except to experts and earnest acolytes. This withdrawal from engagement wasn't merely an ex-pat phenomenon. The suspicions clinging to Wallace Stevens (who never left the country) is and has been more along the lines that he is guilty of an ethical violation: he barely mentions either of the two major wars that bookend his career. Is this evidence of a lack of a social conscience? Marianne Moore's connection to global history seems to have exhausted itself in one early poem, "The Fish," which is apparently about a warship torpedoed by a German U-boat during World War I. Hart Crane, the joy of one's youth, never mentions politics or contemporary history, even in his wonderful letters, and touches on contemporary cultural figures only twice ("Chaplinesque" and "Sunday Morning Apples," in *White Buildings*). Williams becomes vocally "political" only after World War II, and then only in opposition to the *Pisan*

Cantos being awarded the Bollingen. And then there is Yeats. The greatest poet to write in English in the 20th century was obsessed with politics, but only those of Ireland, and even then, only those that threatened the Irish ascendancy. The obsession matured into the anti-humanist fascism of his late plays and the truly ugly late pamphlet, *On the Boiler*.

My list is hardly comprehensive, but comprehensiveness is a nuisance when you face the obvious: Modernism has finally withered into what it always was, a resurrected neo-classicism that championed the rational against unreason in any form and that wanted nothing to do with living history. "Unreason" meant the Freudian subconscious: when confronted with the role played by the "unconscious" in poetry, Eliot had reverted to wisecracks ("the bad poet is usually unconscious where he ought to be conscious, and conscious where he ought to be unconscious"). "Unreason" also implied Coleridge's Primary Imagination and Whitman's dismissals of history's "creeds and schools." In their places were the Imagist manifesto and the elevation of abstractions like *tradition*, *depersonalization*, and *technique*. In some too-obvious ways, this need to make an end run around High Romantic poetry and the revolutionary politics of the Shelleys and Byrons explains the mischievous politics of the major players—the philosophical quietism of Crane, Pound's and Yeats's fascism, Eliot's royalism, even Stevens' ambivalence—and the undecidable political stands of others. But clearly, Modernism's go-to method of capturing the past—Pound's definition of an epic was "a poem that includes history" —was to reconstitute it as myth, rather than playing it back unfiltered, through direct personal experience. When Pound finally is forced to do just that, in the *Pisan Cantos*, it's only after he had been incarcerated for nearly a month in a six-by-six steel mesh cage, in Pisa, which led to a nervous breakdown.

As a result, American Modernism's arrogation of the word *modern* is something of a bad joke. Robert Graves, who gave the movement its name in the mid-twenties, did so not only ironically but with deep loathing, noting specifically that *The Waste Land* had little or nothing directly to say about the context of its actual composition and later bitchily wondering aloud what Eliot was up to while Graves was being wounded at the Battle of the Somme. Sour grapes, perhaps, but Graves had a point, and Modernism's deadpan formalist aesthetic and alienation from the experience of dog-and-cat humanity would dominate poetry in America into the Fifties. The country had to wait for the Beats and a generation that included not only Plath and Lowell but Dugan, Baraka, and Ammons to read poems about hanging drywall, diapering babies, and waking up after a series of electroshock treatments. Between 1920 and 1950, there were, of course, some luminous exceptions—Gwendolyn Brooks's *Annie Allen* (1949), William Carlos Williams' experimental *Paterson*—but homegrown American poetry seemed a tourist of its own contemporaneity; rhetorically incapacitated, if not openly hostile to talking about it. Between the wars only the novelists—Steinbeck, DosPassos, Fitzgerald, Hurston—seemed politically engaged; the single American veteran of World War I who wrote about that experience was a Red Cross ambulance driver, Hemingway. Except for outliers like the Harlem Renaissance group and writers on the socialist or communist or aesthetic fringe, no American poet seemed to be paying attention to global or national politics.

Prévert's *Paroles*, published at mid-century, embraced everything that our partly homegrown, partly cosmopolitan Modernism dismissed. Still gaining its due share of cisatlantic readers, who are learning late what French school-kids grow up with, and grow up memorizing, its importance is probably greater now than at any time since its publication nearly seventy years ago. These poems are first to last politically aware, culturally engaged, and, in contrast to any of the examples just produced, stripped of appeals to mythic orders or to a supposititious "Tradition" that, for Eliot and the New Critics who promoted him, was Pauline Christianity in aesthetic drag. Prévert's poems break rules; they insist that we pay attention to the men behind the curtain—the exploiters, bullies, liars and cheats—as well as to those they exploit, like the homeless vagrants sleeping on park benches ("Le Désespoir est assis sur un banc"). His poetry has no patience with abstractions or the those infatuated with them. They're filled with puns—*puns*, and not bilingual ones like those of Pound in *Mauberley*—and they play fast and loose not only with ordinary words but with the reputations of the powerful. The powerful also engage in wordplay, their wordplays are rarely enjoyable and usually lethal.

So perhaps the strongest summary of Prévert's difference from American verse is this: of the major works by Americans up to 1949, the year that *Paroles* appeared, *The Four Quartets*, *The Cantos*, and that loveable but failed epic, *The Bridge*, not one successfully "reads" the past, narrates current events, or finds an audience wider than the impressed members of American academy. Williams was the exception, but *Paterson* attempts to incorporate contemporary events through a collage method that Williams, a lyrical poet at heart, a sprinter and not a marathoner, never entirely mastered. The stories they told were either redirected through and dominated by refined classical mannerisms, or, in the case of *Paterson*, overwhelmed by the sheer wealth of unassimilated information. The actual present was either not treated as legitimate history or deemed clutter, excrescence, something always in the way, so novel and "reportable" that it had to be celebrated in overwrought, dated idiolects.

For an American reader raised in the crypto-religion of the New Criticism, Prévert was on first encounter a confusing comedian, even a vulgarian, before he got a chance to mature into an refreshing alternative to what one grew up with. In my teens I found him simply "too easy" compared to classy Valéry, dangerous Rimbaud, or the Delphic, unapproachable Mallarmé. He was formally shapeless when held up against Baudelaire, Verlaine, or even Apollinaire. He came across as irreverent, angry, profane, and too easily seduced by available wordplay—the dinner partner who can't resist a bad pun. Even though he is a committed ironist, his favored mode is sarcasm, which is usually called the lowest form of irony because it is the ironic register we first learn as children. He seems never to have heard of myth or the "mythic method"; the closer he gets to the traditional or the classical, the more he seems bored with it, or gently parodies it. His French is idiomatic, easy to "get"; he takes things personally, has political views; and crucially, like all strong lyric voices, he has an eye for what is overlooked. O'Hara's cry, "It's my duty to be attentive, I am needed by things as the sky must be above the earth," is the job description of the lyric poet: you're here to notice the little things—from that homeless veteran to the runaway teenager shivering in the middle of Place de la Concorde on (of all dates!) 15 August, the Feast of the Assumption of the Blessed Virgin, and one of the Roman Catholic Church's Holy Days of Obligation.

Prévert is also a wonderful raconteur, somebody you would love to have dinner or a drink with. He knows how and when to get out of the way of a good story and allow a reader to fill in the blanks ("Le Message"). Second only to Joyce's own profane version in the "Cyclops" chapter of *Ulysses*, his "Pater Noster" is the consummate parody of the prayer the faithful recite Saturday in the confessional or on Sunday before the Doxology. (In season five of *The Sopranos*, Meadow Soprano recites the poem in translation to her father.) Modernism carried its avoidance of clichés so far that it nearly succeeds in avoiding the vernacular entirely; the result is often bracing and new, but when it is not, the results can be disastrous—the pedantry of the *Cantos*, for instance, or the sentimentality of the overpraised *Four Quartets*. Cliché is mass response mass-reproduced. It is the soul of the greeting card, whose bleeding heart is commodified feeling, language industrialized by commerce and weaponized by government. Clichés survive because they resist correction and because we are too busy or lazy to examine the premises of its phrasings—*moral compass,* for instance, suggests that there exists a moral North Pole, which, if you press too hard, you're testily reminded is the Bible. The cliché is like a junk bond; its perfection is perfection of the lowest order; the system would collapse without it. Nothing can compete with a cliché because the competition is fixed.

Prévert understood the workings of the cliché industry and despised how clichés are deployed to control populations. Yet he never seems to have met a cliché he could not turn inside-out, or a wordplay he didn't like. Prévert is so defiantly in love with freewheeling wordplay and verbal mugging that the result sometimes defeats translation. When he embraces one, it's in order to expose and exploit the messiness of language, always and everywhere, and sometimes even in the same poem. "Presque," a meditation on the concurrence of good and bad in the world, goes out of its way to dramatize its point by using the antonyms *bonheur* and *malheur,* roughly "goodness" and "badness," in the same poem:

Presque[*]

A Fontainebleau
Devant l'hôtel de l'Aigle Noir
Il y a un taureau sculpté par Rosa Bonheur
Un peu plus loin tout autour
Il y a la forêt
Et un peu plus loin encore
Joli corps
Il y a encore la forêt
Et le malheur
Et tout à côté le bonheur
Le bonheur avec les yeux cernés
Le bonheur avec des aiguilles de pin dans le dos
Le bonheur qui ne pense à rien

---

[*] Translated on page 37.

Le bonheur comme le taureau
Sculpté par Rosa Bonheur
Et puis le malheur
Le malheur avec une montre en or
Avec un train à prendre
Le malheur qui pense à tout ...
A tout
A tout ... à tout ... à tout ...
Et à tout
Et qui gagne "presque" à tous les coups
Presque.

Rosa Bonheur was a 19th-century artist and sculptor renowned for her representations of animals. Her country estate in Fontainebleau, where she lived and worked, was turned into a museum dedicated to her work after her death. To Prévert, however, it is her surname as much as her art (*un taureau sculpté par Rosa Bonheur*) that is essential to the poem's operations. The paired antonyms do double duty as they build the nucleus. The products of what is good, like the work of Bonheur, exist side by side with what is bad. No matter how "good" a work of art is or how successfully it meets its aesthetic goals, "good" and "bad" carry on necessary existential lives in the real world. Moreover, they live in close proximity, almost touching. The poem's title is expressive of both irony and frustration: good and evil not only coexist but cohabit nearly (*presque*) the same spaces (*Et le malheur / Et tout à côté le bonheur*).

There is a story behind the poem. At one point in his career, Prévert retired to the hotel to complete a screenplay; the poem is a reflection on that sabbatical, not only from Paris but from his mistress, who seems to be the "Joli corps" of line seven. Looking outward from a window in the hotel towards the woods beyond, Prévert imagines the girl he loves lying on the forest floor and looking up at him. Whether she is there in the flesh or not is hardly the point; it's the proximity of the visionary to the actual, the fact that vision and reality *nearly* touch, that creates the pathos. At one stage in my translating this poem I tried to reproduce in English the ironic doubling of proper name and abstract quality, of *bonheur / malheur*; I substituted Wright, as in Frank Lloyd, for Bonheur and Taliesen for Fontainebleau; I even discovered a Wright sculpture, *Boulder*, that might pair with the poem's sculpted bull. The result was not pretty. I bring it up only to suggest the range of untranslatable wordplay in the poem; it's nearly dead on the page.†

The poem is a Blakean lesson in seeing "not with but through the eye." The more alert and attentive we are, the more the world's symmetries seem apparent; this alertness extends to language at the molecular level of puns, double entendres, even homonyms and near synonyms (*bonheur* and *malheur*). Even at its most alert, the mind patiently and proudly peels ideas apart, but the world refuses to follow, and wherever we go we encounter one more example of language and its frustrated intellectual dominance of the sensuous realm. The result is lyric, which is our living out of our own ambiguities, where each line of verse is how the living can gain some sense of the meaning of *duration*, or what endures.

Prévert the late-Modernist was a notable if unconscious dissenter from the the twentieth century's elevation of art to the alienating position assumed by its masterpieces. He was also cool to the idea of the intellect as an unambiguously positive cultural value or, in the words from Aristotle quoted by Eliot in part III of "Tradition and the Individual Talent," that the mind is "immortal

---

† In my defense, "Joli corps," literally "beautiful body," is stripped of a definite or indefinite article and therefore an unconventional noun-adjective dyad; you would normally expect an article to precede the adjective. My research also led me to a strain or family of French bulls apparently named *Joli Corps*. Just as (Rosa) Bonheur and *malheur* are coequal and coexistent opposites, so too are the bronze bull housed outside the hotel and some real bull out pastured near the forest, its lovely body (*joli corps*) the latest to emerge from a famous lineage ("Joli Corps"). I've been unable to find the source of that earlier "discovery."

and immune to suffering." In my late teens, this made Prévert and his poems seem merely silly. Yeats was anti-intellectual, Pound a pseudo-intellectual, but Prévert struck me as simply silly. Many decades later, I think it more accurate to say that his view of the intellectual life was a product of the worst war the world has ever seen, and therefore both witheringly skeptical of platitudes and critical of those who get away with them. Where the intelligence errs, as he argues in "On ne faut pas" ("The 11th Commandment"), is in the way it habitually peels facts from values, ideas from applications, concepts from actions, even people from their words. His most exacting revelations invite flatfooted wordplays, as if to be human is to be part Cumaean Sibyl and part Daffy Duck—ludic, confusing, teasing, silly, and if ambiguous, productively so. At times the wordplays look less like windows into revelation than traps for pretension. Puns amuse (even when we don't laugh at them) because they suggest a world so perforated with falseness and accident that tragi-comedy is always waiting to happen, especially when the wisdom-spouters tend to be blind to the possibility that facts can change, that histories should be written on perforated pages, that truth and lie not only coexist but sometimes *sound* nearly the same.

Poems that embrace the vernacular and its hit-and-run energy may also openly court vulgarity. What's impressive is that Prévert's poems do so, usually, without celebrating vulgarity, or without vulgar stridency. Like Picasso and Cocteau's cocktail-napkin masterpieces, a poem by Prévert can represent the instantaneous with an attentive, but tentative vitality. "La Belle Saison" contains a whole dossier of unpacked implications:

La Belle Saison‡

À jeun perdue glacée
Toute seule sans un sou

---

‡ Translated on page 4.

> Une fille de seize ans
> Immobile debout
> Place de la Concorde
> À midi le Quinze Août

Who is this young woman? A waif, a prostitute? The implied detail—that she's probably panhandling and hungry, and that it's mid-August and she's cold—has to be teased out. The taut, freeze-frame immediacy is the visual signature of 20th-century literary technique and the now-overworked "show, don't tell" rule. And something more: in a bare six lines, he catches a solitary sixteen-year-old's hapless fragility in the middle of one of Europe's most populous and wealthy capitals. She is the homeless kid on a vent on Broadway, cadging change, or nursing a child in the back of Starbuck's. The poem's cinematic concision reminds you that Prévert wrote screenplays. He may also be betraying the influence of Apollinaire—Apollinaire's "L'Adieu" is the same length—another spokesman for the surly but necessary untidiness of human language, which is most messy when it is most true. The difference is that Apollinaire was a diehard formalist and never seems at ease with details that demand a flat, plainspoken rendering. Prévert's formal engagements seem in contrast one-night stands, welcomed when successful, broken off when not. The essence of a Prévert lyric is that *any* moment contains *only* itself, and the poem's work is to make you experience our own hapless duration—the time it takes to speak the words that take us to the end of his line is how we experience that illusory sense of our permanence in the world. It is the quality of wild and unwilled spontaneity that Americans value in Whitman and Dickinson, and in the 20th century, in poets as different as Williams, Ammons, Crane, and the Plath of *Ariel*. It is exactly not, on the other hand, what we tend to value in quick-takes like Pound's lovely but entirely fake haiku, "In a Station of the Metro," where the human element is absorbed first into a "crowd" and then translated into "petals." People are seen from a train platform, then from twenty thousand feet. But who are they?

Prévert's work places huge value on the human, the personal, to the point where it may track into sentiment. It was "Confessional" two decades before confessionalism became a term of abuse for poetic over-sharing, in the late 1960s, and so obviously "performative" the Beats found it irresistibile (yet it survives on the page, as *text*). He wrote about everything: drunken plumbers, career losers, snails, an emperor, florists, gorgeous women, runaway kids, Hitler, and the Blessed Trinity. He was never squeamish when it came to adopting testy or cumbersome *personae*, and excepting those poems where his rage overcomes him ("L'Effort humain"), his sense of humor is vigilant and refuses the specifications of ideology. In "Il ne faut pas," he carries on his debate with abstraction and its lethal consequences by exploiting how the French words for *lie* and *intellectual* (*mentir* and *mental*) have the same root and thus might appear to be cognate, though they are not. It's no wonder he was constantly "speaking truth to power": he had survived the German Occupation, that earlier post-truth epoch, as well as a Catholic-school education. When the powerful act in ways that exceed our ability to satirize them, the last resort is to use the language of exploitation against itself. It is the way adolescents learn resistance: you mirror the authoritarian and his habitual distortions of common, everyday terms by inverting and turning those distortions inside out. You turn the mirror on itself. Published so soon after World War II, *Paroles* denounced all gloriously worded abstractions. It is the book that established his reputation as a partisan of truth informed by his experience of everything, including politics; it is what used to be called, unhelpfully, "protest poetry."

The importance of Prévert's work was at first circumscribed, especially in America, not only because of its Lefty politics but also by its stylistic wildness. It got to these shores a bit late, and at a moment when our poetry had surrendered to the aesthetic conservative's pretense that *The Waste Land* was about World War I and not Eliot's marriage, and that the density of the *Cantos* or of the typical lyric in *White Buildings* had nothing to do with Pound's routine misreading of history or Crane's need to disguise his sexuality. His influence grew through the Fifties, in part because the Beats, and particularly one of his best translators, Lawrence Ferlinghetti, seem to have learned something important from him. Seventy years on, his work recovers some of the immediacy it had when it first appeared. It is *populist* in the most authentic sense, not associated with demagoguery or the bogus, two-headed idealism that now surrounds us. Prévert's politics were always of the Left, and his poetry is vaguely "socialist-inspired," but it is never *simply* that. At its core it has the character of all important lyric—speech that "punches up" and unflattens the world, speech felt "along the pulse," as Keats said. It is language that holds the world close and keeps it there for as long it takes for you to recognize how briefly we embrace it.

*

Translation for poets is always a form of self-deliverance, self-reflection and always improvisation. The early twentieth century went to translation school with Pound, and learned, through his experiments with the Latin and the Chinese, that a good translation need not be as literal or as dull as a trot or the Loeb classics. Pound's example argues that translation—especially for poets—is an act of interpretation and, if less than colonization or corporate takeover, a conversation with another text that is a critique as well as a celebration. This is the approach I have taken in these versions of Prévert. Not a professional translator, I approach the poems as a poet who not only comes after Prévert but whose translations are often improvisations, modeled "after" the originals—whence my title. My occasional updating of references will be obvious (as, for instance, in "Presque" and "La Grasse Matinée") and justified either by my desire to avoid anachronism or save the reader the nuisance of doing research I have already done. The beauty of a bilingual edition is that it liberates a readership to make its own decisions about a translator's decisions; the presence of endnotes adds another layer of utility. Where I found myself stranded between bleak literalness or bleaker pizzazz, I have tried to avoid both, in one or two instances giving the literal translation in my note. Ferlinghetti's versions, produced over forty years ago, in some ways really cannot be improved upon for their accuracy, but a translation should strive for more than literal accuracy and must always be more than a public service announcement, and Prévert's music, and the suddenly alarming and insistent note of his rage and anguish, absolutely demands a revisit.

After Prévert:
Poems from *Paroles* (1949)

La Belle Saison

À jeun perdue glacée
Toute seule sans un sou
Une fille de seize ans
Immobile debout
Place de la Concorde
À midi le Quinze Août.

Nice Weather

Hungry spaced-out shivering
Alone broke
She's sixteen a runaway
Upright immobile
Middle of the intersection Place de la Concorde
Lunchtime 15 August[1]

Pater Noster

Notre Père qui êtes aux cieux,
Restez-y!
Et nous nous resterons sur la terre
Qui est quelquefois si jolie
Avec ses mystères de New York
Et puis ses mystères de Paris
Qui valent bien celui de la Trinité
Avec son petit canal de l'Ourcq
Sa grande muraille de Chine
Sa rivière de Morlaix
Ses bêtises de Cambrai
Avec son océan Pacifique
Et ses deux bassins aux Tuileries
Avec ses bons enfants et ses mauvais sujets
Avec toutes les merveilles du monde
Qui sont là
Simplement sur la terre
Offertes à tout le monde
Eparpillées
Emerveillées elles-mêmes d'être de telles merveilles
Et qui n'osent se l'avouer
Comme une jolie fille nue qui n'ose pas se montrer
Avec les épouvantables malheurs du monde
Qui sont légion
Avec leurs légionnaires
Avec leurs tortionnaires
Avec les maîtres de ce monde
Les maîtres avec leurs prêtres leurs traîtres et leurs reîtres

Avec les saisons
Avec les années
Avec les jolies filles et avec les vieux cons
Avec la paille de la misère pourrissant l'acier des canons.

Pater Noster

Our Father That art in Heaven
Stay there
We're doing just fine
Earth is not such a bad place
Compared, I mean, to the eight million stories in the Naked City
Or the beauties of Paris
Who needs the Trinity?[2]
Next to the Suez Canal
Or the Great Wall
The Nile or the Amazon
Godiva Chocolates
Or *El Niño* the Pacific Ocean?
So much to see, to know, to learn
About plain old low-down Earth
So many surprises
Scattered all over
Amazed by our amazement
We may be too reluctant to say so
Like the young sodalist too modest to walk around naked
And even granting the world's shocking evils
And granting the legions and habitués of horror
I'll take the habitués and the sons of habitués
Who feed on terror
The torturers
The Pols and the Pol Pots the Hitlers Stalins Trumps
Bullies quislings punks reality show creeps

And those poor pretty young thangs who hang out with old farts
Whose misery is the soured distillate of a billion blowhards[3]

Le Discours sur la paix

Vers la fin d'un discours extrêmement important
le grand homme d'Etat trébuchant
sur une belle phrase creuse
tombe dedans
et désemparé la bouche grande ouverte
haletant
montre les dents
et la carie dentaire de ses pacifiques raisonnements
met à vif le nerf de la guerre
la délicate question d'argent.

Toothless Argument

Toward the end of an "extremely critical address"
the Secretary of State stepped into
a perfectly empty phrase
and fell face first
his big mouth wide open
gasping
breaking a tooth
opening the cavity in his argument
and exposing the live nerve of *war*
in that touchy reference to *oil*

La Grasse Matinée

Il est terrible
le petit bruit de l'œuf dur cassé sur un comptoir d'étain
il est terrible ce bruit
quand il remue dans la mémoire de l'homme qui a faim
elle est terrible aussi la tête de l'homme
la tête de l'homme qui a faim
quand il se regarde à six heures du matin
dans la glace du grand magasin
une tête couleur de poussière
ce n'est pas sa tête pourtant qu'il regarde
dans la vitrine de chez Potin
il s'en fout de sa tête l'homme
il n'y pense pas
il songe
il imagine une autre tête
une tête de veaux par exemple
avec une sauce de vinaigre
ou une tête de n'importe quoi qui se mange
et il remue doucement la mâchoire
doucement
et il grimace des dents doucement
car le monde se paye sa tête
et il ne peut rien contre ce monde
et il compte sur ses doigts un deux trois
un deux trois
cela fait trois jours qu'il n'a pas mangé
et il a beau se répéter depuis trois jours
ça ne peut pas durer
ça dure

trois jours
trois nuits
sans manger
et derrières ces vitres
ces pâtés ces bouteilles ces conserves
poissons morts protégés par les boîtes
boîtes protégées par les vitres
vitres protégées par les flics
flics protégés par la crainte
que de barricades pour six malheureuses sardines …
Un peu plus loin le bistrot
café-crème et croissants chauds
l'homme titube

et dans l'intérieur de sa tête
un brouillard de mots
un brouillard de mots
sardines à manger
œuf dur café-crème
café arrosé rhume
café-crème
café-crème
café-crime arrosé sang !…
Un homme très estimé dans son quartier
a été égorgé en plein jour
l'assassin le vagabond lui a volé deux francs
soit un café arrosé
zéro francs soixante dix
deux tartines beurrées

et vingt-cinq centimes pour le pourboire du garçon.
Il est terrible le petit bruit de l'œuf dur cassé sur un comptoir
      d'étain
Il est terrible ce bruit
quand il remue dans la mémoire de l'homme qui à faim.

Continental Breakfast

It hurts
the sound of a hard-boiled egg
being peeled on a plate
It hurts, just the sound
stirs the memory of a hungry man
His head hurts
it too starves
staring at a menu in a diner window
at 9 in the morning
head gray as dust

He is not looking at himself
in the glass
He's too fed up with that face
though he doesn't think
he dreams
imagines another head
a pig's head
vinegar sauce
a head you can eat
he grinds his teeth
slobbers

The world fills his head
he can't eat the world
he counts on his fingers
one two three
days since he's eaten
he's been counting off the days to himself

three whole days

It can't go on
can it
It does
three days
no food
behind the window
pâtés preserves
unhappy sardines
safe behind glass
behind bars
behind fear
all this protection
for a crate of sad sack sardines

Up the street there's a deli
his hunger, staggering
his head, a dream-stew
sardines patés hard boiled
eggs filets salami lox
coffee with rum
with cream
cream
cappuccino
rum-infused latté
with cream coffee with
crime
blood-infused

A tourist midtown
Mugged in broad daylight
Vagrant got off
With traveler's checks

and a buck eighty-seven,
enough for a Tall black coffee
plus a buttered scone
maybe a tip
definitely not

It hurts
the whisper of a hard-boiled egg
peeled on a plate
it hurts, it stirs
the hungry appetite of a hungry man

Chanson des escargots qui vont à l'enterrement

A l'enterrement d'une feuille morte
Deux escargots s'en vont
Ils ont la coquille noire
Du crêpe autour des cornes
Ils s'en vont dans le soir
Un très beau soir d'automne
Hélas quand ils arrivent
C'est déjà le printemps
Les feuilles qui étaient mortes
Sont toutes ressuscitées
Et les deux escargots
Sont très désappointés
Mais voilà le soleil
Le soleil qui leur dit
Prenez prenez la peine
La peine de vous asseoir
Prenez un verre de bière
Si le cœur vous en dit
Prenez si ça vous plaît
L'autocar pour Paris
Il partira ce soir
Vous verrez du pays
Mais ne prenez pas le deuil
C'est moi qui vous le dit
Ça noircit le blanc de l'œil
Et puis ça enlaidit
Les histoires de cercueils
C'est triste et pas joli

Reprenez vous couleurs
Les couleurs de la vie
Alors toutes les bêtes
Les arbres et les plantes
Se mettent à chanter
A chanter à tue-tête
La vrai chanson vivante
La chanson de l'été
Et tout le monde de boire
Tout le monde de trinquer
C'est un très joli soir
Un joli soir d' été
Et les deux escargots
S'en retournent chez eux
Ils s'en vont très émus
Ils s'en vont très heureux
Comme ils ont beaucoup bu
Ils titubent un p'tit peu
Mais là-haut dans le ciel
La lune veille sur eux.

Did You Hear the One About

Two snails go to the funeral of
an autumn leaf,
head off in black tails,
horns wrapped in black crepe,
into the October night, and what
a beautiful fall night but
whoa! By the time they get there
it's already spring
the dead leaves are green
and our two snails are devastated
but the spring sun says

Easy does it, calm down,
sit yourselves down
grab a beer
whatever you want
then catch the Paris bus
it leaves tonight
and see the country
but leave your grief here!
This comes from the top
grief whitens the eyes
then uglifies them
tales from the tomb are gravid, unpleasant
Put your colors back on
wear the colors of life

Then all the beasts
The trees and plants

Struck up a song
A real summer song
And everything drank
And all got drunk
What a shindig
A beautiful summer night
And the two snails
Went home deeply moved, happy even
And so drunk
They wobbled a bit
But above in the sky
The old moon escorted them home

Le Cancre

Il dit non avec la tête
Mais il dit oui avec le cœur
il dit oui à ce qu'il aime
il dit non au professeur
il est debout
on le questionne
et tous les problèmes sont posés
soudain le fou rire le prend
et il efface tout
les chiffres et les mots
les dates et les noms
les phrases et les pièges
et malgré les menaces du maître sans
sous les huées des enfants prodiges
avec des craies de toutes les couleurs
sur le tableau noir du malheur il
dessine le visage du bonheur

Class Clown

He shakes his head *no*
but his heart sighs *yes*
to the things that he loves
He says no to the teacher
he is told to stand up
he is overwhelmed by the question
and bursts out laughing
and with his palm erases
the numbers and words
the dates and names
phrases and riddles
the smart kids love it
the teacher is pissed
but he ignores them
teachers students
and with the colored chalk
all over those angry blackboards
over *allegory* and *crusaders* and *king*
and all those unsmiling faces
draws red and yellow
happy faces
all smiling
all saying *yes*

Il ne faut pas ...

Il ne faut pas laisser les intellectuels jouer avec les allumettes
Parce que Messieurs quand on le laisse seul
Le monde mental Messssieurs
N'est pas du tout brillant
Et sitôt qu'il est seul
Travaille arbitrairement
S'érigent pour-soi-même
Et soi-disant généreusement en l'honneur des travailleurs du bâtiment
Un auto-monument
Répétons-le Messssssieurs
Quand on le laisse seul
Le monde mental
Ment
Monumentalement

11ᵗʰ Commandment

Never let intellectuals play with matches:
People! when it's left on its own
the groping intellect
can't find the switch
when it is left on its own
it works mindlessly
and "out of generosity for our noble
labor movement"
makes a mess of its mission
so
repeat after me:
when it's left on its own
the mind will produce
monumentally
mindless
mendacities

Le Désespoir est assis sur un banc

Dans un square sur un banc
Il y a un homme qui vous appelle quand on passe
Il a des binocles un vieux costume gris
Il fume un petit ninas il est assis
Et il vous appelle quand on passe
Ou simplement il vous fait signe
Il ne faut pas le regarder
Il ne faut pas l'écouter
Il faut passer
Faire comme si on ne le voyait pas
Comme si on ne l'entendait pas
Il faut passer et presser le pas
Si vous le regardez
Si vous l'écoutez
Il vous fait signe et rien personne
Ne peut vous empêcher d'aller vous asseoir près de lui
Alors il vous regarde et sourit
Et vous souffrez atrocement
Et l'homme continue de sourire
Et vous souriez du même sourire
Exactement
Plus vous souriez plus vous souffrez
Atrocement
Plus vous souffrez plus vous souriez
Irrémédiablement
Et vous restez là
Assis figé
Souriant sur le banc
Des enfants jouent tout près de vous

Des passants passent
Tranquillement
Des oiseaux s'envolent
Quittant un arbre
Pour un autre
Et vous restez là
Sur le banc
Et vous savez vous savez
Que jamais plus vous ne jouerez
Comme ces enfants
Vous savez que jamais plus vous ne passerez
Tranquillement
Comme ces passants
Que jamais plus vous ne vous envolerez
Quittant un arbre pour un autre
Comme ces oiseaux.

Park Bench Sphinx

Any neighborhood park bench
That man who calls out as you pass
Bifocals beat-up wool suit
Chewed cigar stub
Never gets up
Just yells after you
Or makes some sign—

Whatever you do
Don't look
Don't listen
Keep going
Act like you never saw him
Never heard him
Walk faster
Pretend one of you's invisible
Or else if you give in
Look
Or listen
He will do this special thing and
                              then nothing on earth
Will be able to stop you from taking a seat beside him

Then he will look into you and smile
And hideously you will suffer hideously
And he will just keep on smiling
And soon you will be smiling his smile
And the more you smile the more horribly
It will hurt

The more it hurts the more you will smile
Smile!
And there you are
Smiling away!
At children playing so close, so close you can smell their diapers
At passersby
Casually
At the birds circling
And leaving one tree for another
And there you are finally
Benched
And you know,
You know for sure

Never again will you play
Like these kids
Never again stroll contentedly
Like these passersby
Never follow again with clear eyes
The free-wheeling birds

Page d'écriture

Deux et deux quatre
quatre et quatre huit
huit et huit seize …
Répétez ! dit le maître
Deux et deux quatre
quatre et quatre huit
huit et huit font seize
Mais voilà l'oiseau-lyre
qui passe dans le ciel
l'enfant le voit
l'enfant l'entend
l'enfant l'appelle :
Sauve-moi
joue avec moi
oiseau !
Alors l'oiseau descend
et joue avec l'enfant
Deux et deux quatre …
Répétez ! dit le maître
et l'enfant joue
l'oiseau joue avec lui …
Quatre et quatre huit
huit et huit font seize
et seize et seize qu'est-ce qu'ils font ?
Ils ne font rien seize et seize
et surtout pas trente-deux
de toute façon
et ils s'en vont.
Et l'enfant a caché l'oiseau

dans son pupitre
et tous les enfants
entendent sa chanson
et tous les enfants
entendent la musique
et huit et huit à leur tour s'en vont
et quatre et quatre et deux et deux
à leur tour fichent le camp
et un et un ne font ni une ni deux
un à un s'en vont également.
Et l'oiseau-lyre joue
et l'enfant chante
et le professeur crie :
Quand vous aurez fini de faire le pitre !
Mais tous les autres enfants
écoutent la musique
et les murs de la classe
s'écroulent tranquilement.
Et les vitres redeviennent sable
l'encre redevient eau
les pupitres redeviennent arbres
la craie redevient falaise
le porte-plume redevient oiseau.

Copybook Page

2 + 2 = 4
4 + 4 = 8
8 + 8 = 16
Do it again, says Sister Dolores
2 + 2
4 + 4
8 + 8
And the paper Paraclete hung in the window ascends[4]
and one kid sees it
hears it
whistles
Help me
I'm dying
The dove lands
on his pencil end

2 + 2 = 4
Do it again
The boy plays with the bird
the bird with the boy
4 + 4
8 + 8
16 + 16?

Suddenly all numbers vanish
He has perched the bird
on his desk
and it is the end of mathematics
8 + 8 = 0

and 4 + 4 and 2 + 2
pair up like mating birds and fly away
nonplussed the numbers fly off

and the bird plays
and the boy sings
and Sister Dolores of the Sisters of Perpetual Consternation
        intones
Let's have a quiet in here
but the kids have all heard the music
and so have the classroom walls.

They quietly crumble
as the glass devolves into quartz and sand
the ink to octopus blood
the desks to pine trees
                      the chalk to cliffs
blackboard to slate slate to shell
and the pens in the inkwells sprout wings,
        become birds once again

Vous allez voir ce que vous allez voir

Une fille nue nage dans la mer
Un homme barbu marche sur l'eau
Où est la merveille des merveilles
Le miracle annoncé plus haut ?

You'll See Just What You're Going to See

When a naked young woman swims in the sea
while a bearded god walks on its waves,
which is the more miraculous,
which the savior, which one the saved?

J'en ai vu plusieurs

J'en ai vu un qui s'était assis sur le chapeau d'un autre
il était pâle
il tremblait
il attendait quelque chose ... n'importe quoi ...
la guerre ... la fin du monde ...
il lui était absolument impossible de faire un geste ou de
          parler
et l'autre
l'autre qui cherchait « son » chapeau était plus pâle encore
et lui aussi tremblait
et se répétait sans cesse :
mon chapeau...mon chapeau ...
et il avait envie de pleurer.
J'en ai vu un qui lisait les journaux
j'en ai vu un qui saluait le drapeau
j'en ai vu un qui était habillé de noir
il avait un montre
une chaîne de montre
un porte-monnaie
la légion d'honneur
et un pince-nez.
J'en ai vu un qui tirait son enfant par la main
et qui criait ...
j'en ai vu un avec un chien
j'en ai vu un avec une canne à épée
j'en ai vu un qui pleurait
j'en ai vu un qui entrait dans une église
j'en ai vu un autre qui en sortait ...

Outside the V.A. Hospital[5]

I saw one of them sitting on his buddy's hat
he was pale
he trembled
waiting for whatever ... who cares what ...
a war ... the end of the world
totally incapable of motion or speech
and the other
looking for his lost hat was paler still
also trembling
and repeating
My hat where's my fucking hat
on the verge of tears.

One read the paper
one pledged allegiance
another in black
talked to his watch
had a watch chain a money clip a purple heart
and service stripes.
One dragged a child by the hand
and yelled at it
I saw one with a dog
I saw one with a steel cane
one I saw weeping
one entering church
another leaving
and one walked to the top of the street
he seemed to fall off

Presque

À Fontainebleau
Devant l'hôtel de l'Aigle Noir
Il y a un taureau sculpté par Rosa Bonheur
Un peu plus loin tout autour
Il y a la forêt
Et un peu plus loin encore
Joli corps
Il y a encore la forêt
Et le malheur
Et tout à côté le bonheur
Le bonheur avec les yeux cernés
Le bonheur avec des aiguilles de pin dans le dos
Le bonheur qui ne pense à rien
Le bonheur comme le taureau
Sculpté par Rosa Bonheur
Et puis le malheur
Le malheur avec une montre en or
Avec un train à prendre
Le malheur qui pense à tout…
À tout
À tout… à tout… à tout…
Et à tout
Et qui gagne "presque" à tous les coups
Presque.

Almost

At Fontainebleau
In front of a hotel named the Black Eagle
There's a bull sculpted by Rosa Bonheur
A little further on and all around it
Is a forest
And a bit further still
A beautiful body
Surrounded by forest
And evil
So close to the good
Good with its searching eyes
Lying in pine needles
Thinking of nothing at all
Like the bull
Sculpted by Bonheur
Then evil
With its gold watch
With a train to catch
Evil that thinks
of everything
Of ... every ... thing

L'École des beaux-arts

Dans une boîte de paille tressée
Le père choisit une petite boule de papier
Et il la jette
Dans la cuvette
Devant ses enfants intrigués
Surgit alors
Multicolore
La grande fleur japonaise
Le nénuphar instantané
Et les enfants se taisent
Émerveillés
Jamais plus tard dans leur souvenir
Cette fleur ne pourra se faner
Cette fleur subite
Faite pour eux
A la minute
Devant eux.

Instant Art

From a woven Easter basket
Daddy picks up a sphere of confetti
And throws it
Down the toilet
In front of his pop-eyed kids
And it irises
Floridly
Into an instant
Japanese water lily
The kids are shushed
Stunned
And for as long as they live
Their will remember
Spontaneous lilies
Only for them
Only once
For their eyes only

Familiale

La mère fait du tricot
Le fils fait la guerre
Elle trouve ça tout naturel la mère
Et le père qu'est-ce qu'il fait le père?
Il fait des affaires
Sa femme fait du tricot
Son fils la guerre
Lui des affaires
Il trouve ça tout naturel le père
Et le fils et le fils
Qu'est-ce qu'il trouve le fils?
Il ne trouve absolument rien le fils
Le fils sa mère fait du tricot
son père des affaires lui la
guerre
Quand il aura fini la guerre
Il fera des affaires avec son père
La guerre continue la mère continue
elle tricote
Le père continue il fait des affaires
Le fils est tué il ne continue plus
Le père et la mère vont au cimetière
Ils trouvent ça naturel le père et la mère
La vie continue la vie avec le tricot la guerre les affaires
Les affaires la guerre le tricot la guerre
Les affaires les affaires les affaires
La vie avec le cimetière.

All in the Family

Mom's into knitting
Son's into war
Mom thinks he's perfectly normal
And Pop what's Pop into
Money
Pop's into money
Pop figures it's perfectly normal
And Son Son
What does he make of it?
Not a goddamn thing
Mom makes booties Pop makes money Son makes war
When Son's done making war
He'll go into business with Dad
But the war drags on Mom knits and knits
Pop goes about his business
And Son gets killed
Mom and Pop head to Arlington
Saying *Death sucks but it's perfectly normal*
Life goes on with its booties battles profits
Profits battles booties war
Metro to work to sleep[6]
The business of business is business
The business of life is death

Le Retour au pays

C'est un Breton qui revient au pays natal
Après avoir fait plusieurs mauvais coups
Il se promène devant les fabriques à Douarnenez
Il ne reconnaît personne
Personne ne le reconnait
Il est très triste.
Il entre dans une crêperie pour manger des crêpes
Mais it ne peut pas en manger
Il a quelque chose qui les empêche de passer
Il paye
Il sort
Il allume une cigarette
Mail it ne peut pas la fumer.
Il y a quelque chose
Quelque chose dans sa tête
Quelque chose de mauvais
Il est de plus en plus triste
Et soudain it se met à se souvenir:
Quelqu'un lui a dit quand it était petit
"Tu finiras sur l'échafaud"
Et pendant des annees
Il n'a jamais osé rien faire
Pas même traverser la rue
Pas même partir sur la mer
Rien absolument rien
Il se souvient
Celui qui avait tout prédit c'est l'oncle Grésillard
L'oncle Grésillard qui portait malheur a tout le monde
La vache!

Et le Breton pense à sa soeur
Qui travaille a Vaugirard
A son frère mort à la guerre
Pense à toutes les choses qu'il a vues
Toutes les choses qu'il a faites.
La tristesse se serre contre lui
Il essaie une nouvelle fois
D'allumer une cigarette
Mais it n'a pas envie de fumer
Alors il decide d'aller voir l'oncle Gresillard.
Il y va
Il ouvre la porte
L'oncle ne le reconnâit pas
Mais lui le reconnait
Et il lui dit:
      "Bonjour oncle Gresillard"
Et puis il lui tord le cou.
Et il finit sur l'échafaud à Quimper
Après avoir mangé deux douzaines de crêpes
Et fumé une cigarette.

Body Language

A Philadelphian comes home
to his native soil
After a life of lousy luck
Passes the factories in Douarnenez
Recognizes nobody
Nobody recognizes him
Kind of sad.
He enters a bar for breakfast
But can't eat anything
Can't seem to swallow a thing
Pays
Leaves
Lights a cigarette
But can't smoke it.
Something's up
Something's wrong in his head
Something bad
He is sadder and sadder
And gets to remembering
Something an uncle told him when he was a kid:
"You will end up in the electric chair"

It stayed with him for years and years
He remembers how afterward
Too horrified to do anything
He couldn't cross the street
Couldn't drive to the shore
Could do nothing nothing nothing.
He remembers.

The prophet had been an uncle
The whole family had said was only bad luck.

His thoughts drift to his sister
Who works in the city
To his brother, killed in the war,
Then to all the things he'd seen
All the things he had done.
Sadness crowds him
He tries one more time
To light a cigarette
But he has no desire
Except to see that uncle

Off he goes
When he opens the door
His uncle can't recognize him
But he recognizes the uncle
And says to him
"Hey Unk, what's up"
And strangles him
And ends up in the electric chair
After two dozen pancakes
One last cigarette.

Paris at Night

Trois allumettes une à une allumées dans la nuit
La premiére pour voir ton visage tout entier
La seconde pour voir tes yeux
La dernière pour voir ta bouche
Et l'obscurité tout entière pour me rappeler tout cela
En te serrant dans mes bras.

Three on a Match

Three matches struck one. two. three in the night
The first is to see your face all at once
The second your eyes
The third your mouth
Then darkness again to remember it all
And gather you into my arms

Chez la fleuriste

Un homme entre chez une fleuriste
et choisit des fleurs
la fleuriste enveloppe les fleurs
l'homme met la main à sa poche
pour chercher l'argent
l'argent pour payer les fleurs
mais il met en même temps
subitement
la main sur son cœur
et il tombe

En même temps qu'il tombe
l'argent roule à terre
et puis les fleurs tombent
en même temps que l'homme
en même temps que l'argent
et la fleuriste reste là
avec l'argent qui roule
avec les fleurs qui s'abîment
avec l'homme qui meurt
évidemment tout ça est très triste
et il faut qu'elle fasse quelque chose
la fleuriste
mais elle ne sait pas comment s'y prendre
elle ne sait pas
par quel bout commencer

Il y a tant de choses à faire
avec cet homme qui meurt

ces fleurs qui s'abîment
et cet argent
cet argent qui roule
qui n'arrête pas de rouler.

Rolling Poem

Guy stops at the florist's
Valentine's Day
picks out a spray
counter girl wraps it
he sticks his hand in his pocket
pulls out some coin
to pay for his posy
and instantly
claps his hand to his heart
collapses

coins hit floor
flowers follow coins
man follows flowers
the shopto the floor
girl is frozen
the coins roll
the flowers plummet
the man dies

what a mess
must do something
she can't decide
what to do
omigod
so confused
what's what
man dying,
flowers plummeting,

coins rolling
   rolling
   rolling
   rolling

the coins
keep on rolling

Et la fête continue

Debout devant le zinc
Sur le coup de dix heures
Un grand plombier zingueur
Habillé en dimanche et pourtant c'est lundi
Chante pour lui tout seul
Chante que c'est jeudi
Qu'il n'ira pas en classe
Que la guerre est finie
Et le travail aussi
Que la vie est si belle
Et les filles si jolies
Et titubant devant le zinc
Mais guidé par son fil à plomb
Il s'arrête pile devant le patron
Trois paysans passeront et vous paieront
Puis disparaît dans le soleil
Sans régler les consommations
Disparaît dans le soleil tout en continuant sa chanson

Liberation Day

Leaning over the bar
Exactly 10 a.m.
This immense plumber
Dressed for Sunday but it's Monday
Singing his heart out
Belts out *It's Thursday*
School's out War's over
So's work
Life's a blast
And the babes are all beauties
He sways by the sink
Steadied by his plumb-bob
He gets right in the owner's face and says
A couple of my buddies will pick up the tab
Then disappears in the sunshine
Melts into the daylight singing his heart out
Without even leaving a tip

L'Effort humain[7]

L'effort humain
n'est pas ce beau jeune homme souriant
debout sur sa jambe de plâtre
ou de pierre
et donnant grâce aux puérils artifices du statuaire
l'imbécile illusion
de la joie de la danse et de la jubilation
évoquant avec l'autre jambe en l'air
la douceur du retour à la maison
Non
l'effort humain ne porte pas un petit enfant sur l'épaule droite
un autre sur la tête
et un troisième sur l'épaule gauche
avec les outils en bandoulière
et la jeune femme heureuse accrochée à son bras
L'effort humain porte un bandage herniaire
et les cicatrices des combats
livrés par la classe ouvrière
contre un monde absurde et sans lois
L'effort humain n'a pas de vraie maison
il sent l'odeur de son travail
et il est touché aux poumons
son salaire est maigre
ses enfants aussi
il travaille comme un nègre
et le nègre travaille comme lui
L'effort humain n'a pas de savoir-vivre
l'effort humain n'a pas l'âge de raison
l'effort humain a l'âge des casernes

l'âge des bagnes et des prisons
l'âge des églises et des usines
l'âge des canons
et lui qui a planté partout toutes les vignes
et accordé tous les violons
il se nourrit de mauvais rêves
et il se saoule avec le mauvais vin de la résignation
et comme un grand écureuil ivre
sans arrêt il tourne en rond
dans un univers hostile
poussiéreux et bas de plafond
et il forge sans cesse la chaîne
la terrifiante chaîne où tout s'enchaîne
la misère le profit le travail la tuerie
la tristesse le malheur l'insomnie et l'ennui
la terrifiante chaîne d'or
de charbon de fer et d'acier
de mâchefer et de poussier
passée autour du cou
d'un monde désemparé
la misérable chaîne
où viennent s'accrocher
les breloques divines
les reliques sacrées
les croix d'honneur les croix gammées
les ouistitis porte-bonheur
les médailles des vieux serviteurs
les colifichets du malheur
et la grande pièce de musée

le grand portrait équestre
le grand portrait en pied
le grand portrait de face de profil à cloche-pied
le grand portrait doré
le grand portrait du grand divinateur
le grand portrait du grand empereur
le grand portrait du grand penseur
du grand sauteur
du grand moralisateur
du digne et triste farceur
la tête du grand emmerdeur
la tête de l'agressif pacificateur
la tête policière du grand libérateur
la tête d'Adolf Hitler
la tête de monsieur Thiers
la tête du dictateur
la tête du fusilleur
de n'importe quel pays
de n'importe quelle couleur
la tête odieuse
la tête malheureuse
la tête à claques
la tête à massacre
la tête de la peur.

Human Condition

The human condition isn't some grinning good-looking
stud standing on a one leg made of plaster or stone
and creating the idiotic illusion—
thanks to the childish charm of commercial art—
of balletic joy and jubilation
as the other leg rises to mimic
how sweet a thing it is to be home at last

No
the human condition does not carry a child on its right shoulder
another on its back
a third on its left shoulder
while wearing a tool belt
and dangling a giddy young wife on the other arm

The human condition wears a truss
has the battle scars of the underclass
is at war with a lawless world
doesn't own its own home
savors the stink of its own labor
has a touch of black lung
makes lousy money
its kids have lice
works like a slave
it is a slave

The human condition has no "lifestyle"
never experienced an Age of Reason
instead it went through the Age of Barracks

the Age of Penitentiaries and Concentration Camps
Churches and of Factories
Cluster-bombs

It planted vineyards all over the world
tuned all the violins
then fed itself on its own bad dreams
drank itself sick on the wine of resignation
and like a tipsy squirrel
spins nonstop in circles
in a nasty vastness
of dust and low ceilings
It hammers the endless chain
that enchains everything
despair greed work slaughter
wretchedness evil insomnia boredom
terrible gold chain
of cast iron and steel
cinders and dust
hung from the neck
of a world of amputees

Chain of misery
from which dangle
religious trinkets
relics of the saints
Congressional Medals Purple Hearts
goofy good luck charms
Pope bobble heads

good-conduct medals
crap to ward off *malocchio*
and the great museum display
the great equestrian portrait
the great full-body portrait
the great profile of Pharaoh Ramses hopping on one foot
the great gilt portrait
the great fortune teller
the great emperor
the great thinker
the leaper
the moralist
the sick practical joker

The bust of the great paingiver
the head of the passive aggressor
the mug shot of the great liberator
the head of Hitler
the dictator's head
the executioner's head
no matter the country
no matter the color
the same loathsome head
the skinned head of fear

Le Cheval rouge

Dans les manèges du mensonge
Le cheval rouge de ton sourire
Tourne
Et je suis là debout planté
Avec le triste fouet de la réalité
Et je n'ai rien à dire
Ton sourire est aussi vrai
Que mes quatre vérités.

Red Horse Smile

On my dream merry-go-round
There's a red horse with your smile
It goes round and round and
How stilled I am before it
Whipping it back to reality
And with nothing to say
Your smile is proof positive
Of all I have done wrong

Composition Française

Tout jeune Napoléon était très maigre
et officier d'artillerie
plus tard il devint empereur
alors il print du ventre et beaucoup de pays
et le jour où il mourut il avait encore
du ventre
mais il était devenu plus petit

Essay Question

In his youth Napoleon was rather slight
and a mere artillery officer
then he became Emperor
gained lots of territory and weight
and by the time he died
he had lost everything but
the gut[8]

Le Message

La porte que quelqu'un a ouverte
La porte que quelqu'un a refermée
La chaise où quelqu'un s'est assis
Le chat que quelqu'un a caressé
Le fruit que quelqu'un a mordu
La lettre que quelqu'un a lue
La chaise qu quelqu'un a renversée
La porte que quelqu'un a ouverte
La route où quelqu'un traverse
La rivière où quelqu'un se jette
L'hôpital où quelqu'un est mort.

Theory of Narrative

Door open
Door shut
Chair sat in
Cat stroked
Apple bitten
Note read
Chair upset
Door ajar
Road crossed
Woods entered
Bridge guardrail
Splat—The End—

Le Bouquet

Que faites-vous là petite fille
Avec ces fleurs fraîchement coupées
Que faites-vous là jeune fille
Avec ces fleurs ces fleurs séchées
Que faites-vous là jolie femme
Avec ces fleurs qui se fanent
Que faites-vous là vielle femme
Avec ces fleurs qui meurent

J'attends le vainqueur.

Posies

"What are you up to there, little love
With those fresh flowers freshly cut?
What are you up to now, Queen of the May?
Your calla lilies fade and fade.
What are you up to, a mother at last,
Your Mother's Day flowers did not last.
What are you up to now, in that hospice bed,
Your get-well flowers are dying, or dead."

I am getting ready to die.

Riviera

Assise sur une chaise longue
une dame à la langue fanée
une dame longue
plus longue que sa chaise longue
et très âgée
prend ses aises
on lui dit sans doute que la mer était là
alors elle la regarde
mais elle ne la voit pas
et les présidents passent et la saluent très bas
c'est la baronne Crin
la reine de la carie dentaire
son mari c'est le baron Crin
le roi du fumier de lapin
et tous à ses grands pieds sont dans leurs petits souliers
et ils passent devant elle et la saluent très bas
de temps en temps
elle leur jette un vieux cure-dents
ils le sucent avec ravissement
en continuant leur promenade
leurs souliers neufs craquent et leurs vieux os aussi
et des villas arrive une musique blême
une musique aigre
et sure
comme les cris d'un nouveau-né trop longtemps négligé
c'est nos fils
c'est nos fils disent les présidents
et ils hochent la tête doucement et fièrement
et leurs petits prodiges

désespérément
se jettent à la figure leurs morceaux de piano
la baronne prête l'oreille
cette musique lui plaît
mais son oreille tombe
comme une vieille tuile d'un toit
elle regarde par terre
et elle ne la voit pas
mais l'aperçoit seulement
et la prend
tout bonnement
pour une feuille morte apportée par le vent
c'est alors que s'arrête
la triste clameur des enfants
que la baronne n'entendait plus d'ailleurs
que d'une oreille distraite
et dépareillée
et que surgissent brusquement
gambadant dans sa pauvre tête
en toute liberté
les vieux refrains puérils méchants et périmés
de sa mémoire inquiète usée et déplumée
et comme elle cherche vainement
pour passer le temps
qui la menace et qui la guette
un bon regret bien triste et bien attendrissant
qui puisse la faire rire aux larmes
ou même pleurer tout simplement
elle ne trouve qu'un souvenir incongru inconvenant

l'image d'une vieille dame assise toute nue
sur la bosse d'un chameau
et qui tricote méchamment une omelette au guano.

Kicking Back

Stretched out on a deck chair
a woman with a weather-beaten tongue
shaped like a deck chair
longer than the deck chair
and really old
kicks back
she's been told of course of the sea at her feet
which she sees
but doesn't perceive
The VIPs stroll past and lower their voices to say hello
That's Felicia Jumpshot
queen of halitosis
her husband Fuzzy
rabbit-turd king
They scrunch by walking with two feet in one shoe
saying *hello* in lowered voices
and occasionally
she flicks a used toothpick their way
and they snap it up ravenously
and walk on
their new leather cracks, their worn bones crack
and from their seaside villas comes bloodless music
a thin music a music
as sour
as the wails of an infant left crying too long
That's our boy
That's our boy say the VIPs
and they proudly and solemnly nod their heads
at their spoiled prodigies

who desperately
are throwing the sheet music around the room

The baroness takes it in
the music pleases
but her ear blows off
like an old roof tile
that she sees
but doesn't
perceive
she takes it in
vacantly
mistakes it for a leaf tumbled in the wind

whereat the sad sour chopsticks stops
suddenly
and though she lent it only
a detached ear
she finds it unusual
at how abruptly there mounts
and scampers uncontrolled through her empty head

some childhood tease, nasty and dated,
memory-plucked, thought-worn,
and as she casts around vainly
trying to kill time
which is killing her
for the one tender recollection
that would make her laugh till she cries

or simply cry
she has a repulsive vision
of an naked old woman
perched on a camel's hump
working furiously away at a shit sandwich.

Le Combat avec l'ange

N'y va pas
tout est combiné d'avance
le match est truqué
et quand il apparaîtra sur le ring
environné d'éclairs de magnésium
ils entonneront à tue-tête le Te Deum
et avant même que tu te sois levé de ta chaise
ils te sonneront les cloches à toute volée
ils te jetteront à la figure l'éponge sacrée
et tu n'auras pas le temps de lui voler dans les plumes
ils se jetteront sur toi
et il te frappera au-dessous de la ceinture
et tu t'écrouleras
les bras stupidement en croix
dans la sciure
et jamais plus tu ne pourras faire l'amour.

Your Arms Are Too Short to Box with God

Forget about it
the whole thing is fixed
the fight is a scam
and when he shows up in the ring
in a halo of popping flashbulbs
they will roar out a head-splitting *Te Deum*
and even before you can get out of your corner
they will be counting you out
they will toss in the sacred sponge for you
and before you have a chance to get into his kitchen
they will pile on
and he will hit you below the belt
and doubled over
arms stupidly cruciform
you will fall flat on your ass
and forget about making love.

Notes

1. Intentional or not, Prévert's choice of a date is interesting: August 15th is the feast of the Assumption of the Blessed Virgin in France.

2. *Les mystères de New York* is the title of a pulp novel published in the mid-nineteenth century by the American writer Ned Buntline. I've attuned my translation of line 5 to reflect the fact. The phrase "the eight million stories in the Naked City" is itself a reference to the American cops-and-robbers television drama *The Naked City*, pop-cultural pulp of mid-century that seems close in spirit to what Prévert had in mind.

3. Literally, "the straw of misery rotting their cannon's barrels."

4. In Prévert's original, *l'oiseau-lyre* refers to a species of bird whose tail-feathers, in the male, resemble a musical instrument. Representations of the lyre-bird are, I am told, often hung in the classrooms of French grammar schools. The day-dreaming child, the poem implies, gazes at either the lyre-shaped bird passing the window or the bird-shaped instrument hanging above (or in) the window of the classroom, and so his meditation "takes off" from there.

5. Though the poem's title reads literally "I have seen several," my sense throughout is that his subject here is not only the insane vagrants that fill great cities of any age but, and given Prévert's hatred of institutionalized violence, those French Army veterans who were everywhere in Paris right after World War II. Prévert's habit of repeating a phrase, hemi-stitch or a whole line—many commentators have noted it—is not just a habit but a deliberate prosodic invention. It moves his poems at times in the direction of the incantatory and has always struck me as some distant evolutionary outcome of Rimbaud's *Le Bateau Ivre* (with its serial visions, each beginning "I saw ... I saw ...") and, more distantly, John's Apocalypse. The closest we have to it in twentieth-century American poetry is Frank O'Hara's "I-did-this-I-did-that" poems, which constitute the same kind of serious play. The last line is entirely my addition.

6. My thanks to my colleague Jean-Louis Hippolyte for informing me of the French slang saying *métro, boulot, dodo*, of which my line is a rough translation.

7. Ferlinghetti, in his translation of selections from *Paroles* (New Directions, 1990), mentions this poem in his "Translator's Note" but does not include it because he views it as a failure. Prévert, he writes, "begins wonderfully … But he goes on to tell what human effort really is, and we are treated to tritenesses about the low-salaried proletariat," something that "discouraged" Ferlinghetti from finishing his own version.

8. The poem is based on the simple coincidence that the verb *prendre* occurs in several idioms, one of which is *prendre du ventre* (put on weight, grow a potbelly) and another, *prendre beacoup du pays* (to take over a country, grab a lot of territory).

Acknowledgements

Some of these translations have appeared under their present or different titles in the following journals:

Boulevard: "La Grasse Matinee" (as "Continental Breakfast"), "Le Cancre" (as "Class Clown"), "Page d'écriture" (as "Copybook Page"), "L'École des beaux-arts" (as "Art School"), "J'en ai vu plusieurs" (as "Outside the V.F.W. Post"), "Chez la fleuriste" (as "Rolling Poem"), "Et la fête continue" (as "Liberation Day").

The Denver Quarterly: "Le Retour au pays" (as "Body Language").

Plume: "L'Effort humain" (as "The Human Condition").

Subtropics: "Le Désespoir est assis sur un banc" (as "Park Bench Sphinx"), "Chanson des escargots qui vont à l'enterrement" (as "Did You Hear The One About") and "Riviera" (as "Kicking Back").

About Prévert

Jacques Prevért (1900–1977) was well known not only as a poet but a writer of screenplays, most notably for *Les Enfants du Paradis* (1945). A populist from the outset, his work directs its most savage ironies at politicians and grand historical figures who exploit the public. Some of his poems were set to music—covered in America by artists from Nat Cole to Joan Baez to, most recently, Iggy Pop—and achieved a popularity that found their way into the curricula of French schools, some of which bear his name. He published only six books of poetry in his lifetime; *Paroles*, appearing in French in 1946, was his first book and an immediate best-seller. Briefly associated in the late '20s with surrealism, he was involved with the French resistance during the war. His interest in socialist and left-wing politics emerged early in his career and remained with him for the rest of his life.

About the Author

J. T. BARBARESE is a poet and author of six books of poetry and a previous translation of Euripides' *Children of Herakles*. He is also an essayist and fabulist whose literary journalism and fiction has appeared widely.

www.ingramcontent.com/pod-product-compliance
Lightning Source LLC
Chambersburg PA
CBHW020336170426
43200CB00006B/406